ABRAHAM LINCOLN

NATIONAL HERO

THE HISTORY HOUR

CONTENTS

PART I
Introduction — 1

PART II
Abraham Lincoln's Early Days — 3

PART III
The Lincolns Move to Illinois — 7

PART IV
The Lincoln Boys — 25

PART V
The Madness of Mary Lincoln — 37

PART VI
Questionable Rumors About Lincoln — 51

PART VII
Racing Towards Politics — 57

PART VIII
On the Road to the Presidency — 63

PART IX
Wartime politics — 81

PART X
Still Mad Enough to Murder — 89

PART XI
Robert & His Dealings with Mary Todd — 93

PART XII
Lincoln's Final Hours — 99

PART XIII
Conclusion — 109

PART XIV
Further Reading — 115

Your Free eBook! — 117

PART I

INTRODUCTION

∼

Most typical people will look up to Presidents of our country like they are above us, on a pedestal. Maybe not so much today as they did in Lincoln's time, but today we have so much media to broadcast their sins and shortcomings at a minute notice, so we are ready to burn them at stake for the very sins and weaknesses for which many of us are committing ourselves. For this author, the opinion of any sitting President or Congressman is that they were created equal to everyone else.

∼

Abraham Lincoln was the same when he met the people he served. He never felt that he was above anyone.

∼

In this book, you will be able to find out about his lowly beginnings, about his family, how they had to move so often when he was but a lad, how badly he wanted to attend school and how he finally met and married *Mary Todd*.

∼

You will find out about them having four children and what the future held for each of them.

∼

You will find out how Mary Todd Lincoln's insanity affected her, their children and President Lincoln.

∼

You will learn about his climb in political life to President. And you will discover that it was then as it is now, some of the people loved him, and some of them hated him.

∼

You will find out about some of the rumors and gossips attached to Mary and Abraham Lincoln. I will leave it to you in making up your mind as to what you believe.

∼

Please enjoy what this book holds for you.

PART II

ABRAHAM LINCOLN'S EARLY DAYS

«I am a slow walker, but I never walk back.»

Abraham Lincoln

∼

Abraham Lincoln was born into this life on February 12th, 1809 in Kentucky in Hardin County. In 1811, the Lincoln's moved to the Knob Creek Farm. Knob Creek Farm has become part of the Lincoln Birthplace Historic Site. Seven years later, in 1816 the family moved to southern Indiana. His parents, **Nancy Hanks** and **Thomas Lincoln** then had two more children.

∼

Nancy Hanks family tree is hard to follow, but it seems that Nancy was probably illegitimate. She was described as being thin breasted, sad, stoop-shouldered, and very religious.

～

It was after Nancy had died that Tom Lincoln became overwhelmed with caring, farming, and hunting food for his children.

～

If Abraham Lincoln happened to be alive now, he would tell you that his boyhood was the most unhappy part of his life after his biological mother died in the fall of 1818. When Abe was nine years old, he had to watch his beloved mother be buried in the woods, and then face a cold winter without being warmed by his mother's love.

～

It was so bad at times Abe and his sister would be left by themselves, dirty, skinny and beaten by their father. At one time Tom Lincoln abandoned them for six months, but when he came back, he did return with a wife.

～

It was Sarah Bush Johnston Lincoln, a widow that had a boy and two girls she brought with her. Luckily she had lots of energy and much affection to spare. She managed the house with what one would call an unbiased hand because she treated Tom's children and her own as if she had given birth to every one of them. Sarah was very fond of Abraham, and he was fond of her. Later in life, he would reference her as his "***angel mother***."

~

Lincoln's father, Thomas, had come from a line of weaver's apprentices that had migrated from England over to Massachusetts during 1637. Thomas was less than prosperous than some of the other Lincoln's, but he was still a sturdy pioneer with a die-hard attitude.

~

Thomas was Abraham's younger brother, but he expired during infancy. Lincoln had a sister by the name of Sarah, who was older than Abraham.

~

When they moved in 1817, Abraham and his parents relocated to Indiana due to a land dispute. The issue of the land dispute was because it was compounded by all the confusion over all the land grants and the purchase agreements that had been handed out so freely and led to immeasurable legal disputes over all types of land ownership in the state of Kentucky.

~

When the Lincoln's moved to Perry County located in Indiana during 1817 they did "***squat***" some public land. The area they had decided to make their homestead was known to be "***fairly wild***" and a difficult area to farm. It was the cause for Tom Lincoln to hunt so he could feed his family. In this place, Thomas Lincoln built his family a one-room cabin of logs that had no floor and almost no furniture. The entire family slept on bedding made from corn husks.

～

Abraham's earliest memories seem to be those of his childhood home. One special memory was about a flash flood that at one time had come through and washed away all the pumpkin and corn seeds Abraham had just helped his dad, Thomas plant.

～

With hard work and perseverance, Thomas Lincoln eventually earned money to buy that plot of land for his own.

～

There was a period even though brief as it was when a small school was located near the area where they lived, and Abraham Lincoln was said to have walked about nine miles each way to go to school; it was taking two and three hours each way.

～

Abraham Lincoln was self-taught on the law, and when 1836 came to pass, he aced the Law Bar Exam.

PART III

THE LINCOLNS MOVE TO ILLINOIS

«The philosophy of the school room in one generation will be the philosophy of government in the next.»

Abraham Lincoln

~

March of 1830 found the Lincoln family moving again, and this time the move was to Illinois with Lincoln driving the oxen team.

~

Abe had just turned 21 years old and was about to start life on his merit. He was six foot four, gaunt, lean, muscular, and powerful physically. Abe was known for the strength and the skill that he could handle an ax. What woman on the frontier would not be looking for a man such as that?

∽

Abraham had that charming, slow backwoods twang while he walked with a flat-footed, long-stride, cautiously like a plowman would have used. He was good-natured but also moody, very talented in mimicking and telling stories which made him a friend magnet. At this point, he had not demonstrated the other excellent abilities he held.

∽

When Lincoln got to Illinois, he had NO desire to become a farmer, so he tried many occupations. He tried out being a rail splitter, a flatboat man and helped in clearing fences for his father.

∽

While working as a flatboat man, he made his way down the mighty Mississippi to the town of New Orleans in Louisiana. When he returned to Illinois, he decided to settle down in New Salem in a village of about twenty-five other families along the Sangamon River.

∽

In New Salem, he worked as a surveyor, postmaster, and a storekeeper. He knew the Black Hawk War (1832) was coming, so Abe decided to enlist as a volunteer and was immediately elected as the captain of his company.

~

After the fact, Abraham would joke that during the war he had never seen any "*fighting, live Indians*" but his most bloody fights were with mosquitoes.

~

He aspired to be in politics and a legislator but was defeated when he first tried and kept repeating being re-elected for the state assembly. He even considered being a blacksmith for trade but finally decided he wanted to be a lawyer. He had already self-taught himself in mathematics and grammar, and now he was beginning to study the law books. He passed the bar exam in 1836 and started to practice law.

~

The following year he made his move to Springfield, Illinois because it offered so many more chances for a law practice than in New Salem. In the beginning, he formed a partnership with John T. Stuart, then became partners with Stephan T. Logan. In 1844 he worked with William H. Herndon. Herndon was almost ten years younger than Lincoln and was much more read, became more emotional at the bar and what seemed to be more extreme with his views.

~

Lincoln's partnership with Herndon was a little '*fly by night*' as they never kept records for their business. When either of them got paid they just split the cash between the two of them. There is no record of any money quarrels. That would not fly in today's business world on so many levels.

～

After Lincoln had moved to Springfield, he was making $1200 to $1500 each year. At a time when the state governor only received a $1200 yearly, and the circuit judges were making $750. Lincoln had to keep busy; he realized he not only had to work in Springfield but had to stay on the heels of the circuit judge. Every fall and spring Abraham would travel by buggy or horseback for hundreds of miles over prairies that were sparsely settled, going from one county seat to the next. It seemed most of the cases were nothing but petty and the fees for services were small.

～

Once the railroads came through in 1850, it made traveling much easier for Lincoln and others, and his practice began making more money. Lincoln started lobbying for bringing in the Illinois Central Railroad and helped get a charter necessary from the state. After this, the railroad kept Lincoln on retainer as their regular attorney.

～

After Lincoln had defended the Railroad against McLean county for taxing the railroad's property, Lincoln got the most significant single payment during his entire legal career - $5,000. To do this, he had to sue the Railroad to collect. He then began handling cases for banks, other railroads, manufacturing and mercantile firms, and insurance companies.

∼

It was considered one of the most notable highlights of his career when he saved the bridge that spanned the Mississippi River, the Rock Island Bridge, from the threats of the interests that were working on getting the bridge removed. Lincoln's business started to include criminal trials and patent litigation. One of his most famous lawsuits was a murder trial.

∼

There had been a witness who '*claimed*' by the moon's light he had seen a man by the name of Duff Armstrong, supposedly someone that Lincoln knew allegedly had a part in the murder. Lincoln referred to a farmer's almanac to prove that the night was too dark for this witness to be able to see anything explicit. With this sincere appeal that was so moving to the jury, Lincoln won the acquittal.

∼

It was by the time Lincoln started to be prominent on the national political scene, which was about twenty years after becoming a lawyer and noted to be one of the most successful ones in Illinois.

∼

Lincoln seemed to have a unique way about him that

allowed him to be able to see into the heart of any lawsuit but to see the utter honesty and the unwavering fairness even though he was noted for his common sense that seemed so practical but for his understanding as well.

∿

While Abraham Lincoln was living in New Salem, he came to know Ann Rutledge. It seemed he was fond of her, and he grieved as others in the community when she died at the age of 22 in 1835. It appears that after her death, many stories were speculating about the great romance between the two.

∿

There are some who feel that there is no historical evidence that backs any of this up. About a year after Rutledge had passed, Abraham Lincoln started trying to date halfheartedly a Mary Owens. She eventually said that Abe was "***deficient in areas that completed a woman to be happy.***" She supposedly turned down his marriage proposal.

∿

Robert Rutledge, in a letter, started with the storytelling of Ann's engagement to John McNamar followed by quite a colorful drama of Ann having an alleged relationship with Abe Lincoln.

∿

McNamar at the time was a prosperous merchant in New Salem; also a friend of Abraham Lincoln's who had been courting Ann, and had supposedly secured an engagement, and boom! He went back to the east to take care of some family matters. It seemed for some time he wrote letters to Ann, then all of a sudden, the letters stopped coming. It appeared he had left her hanging and publicly embarrassed. Then, appears Lincoln to the rescue.

∽

Robert goes on to say that Abe Lincoln kept visiting Ann, kept giving her attention regularly and it resulted in him asking her to marry him. It was an honorable and conditional release to break the contract with McNamar.

∽

Supposedly, David Rutledge wanted Ann to go ahead and consummate the engagement, but she did not want to do this until she could talk to McNamar face to face. Abe lived there in New Salem and McNamar did not come back until after Ann had died.

∽

It seemed that the effect on Abe Lincoln's mind was horrible, and he went into despair, and so many of his real friends were worried that because of his depression he might lose his mind. Because of his depression and the intense emotions, it seemed strong evidence of Abe's existence of the most tender relationship between Ann Rutledge (the deceased) and himself.

∽

There were Rutledge family members that were firm about the engagement between their sister and Lincoln.

∼

When Ann Rutledge was so ill, Lincoln stayed by her side while she was so sick and dying and then during her burial. Before Ann had become ill, she had agreed to marry Lincoln but consented to wait at least a year before getting married so Abraham could be admitted to the Bar. It was so sad that Ann Rutledge died before the year could pass.

∼

Lincoln was so affected by Anne's death that it seemed the most profound type of melancholy that came over his mind. He kept saying to all his friends:

> 'My heart is buried in the grave with that dear girl.'

Lincoln would often go and sit beside her grave and read the pocket-size Testament he always carried with him.

∼

Once Lincoln became President he felt compelled to answer all the rumors that were circulating about him where others were saying he was an atheist. He sent out an open letter where he stated that he could not support anyone for office that he knew was a public enemy and a scoffer of religion.

'Eternal consequences should be left between each

person and his Divine Maker. No man has any right to insult feelings, injure morals of any community that he lives. If I, Abe Lincoln should be guilty of any such conduct, then I have no right to blame anyone that would condemn me for that; but I would blame those, whoever they might be, that would falsely accuse me of such charge.'

Isaac Cogdal told that Lincoln had admitted how much he loved Ann Rutledge. How he felt she was his first love, the first woman he had loved so sacredly and so dearly; she was a beautiful girl and would have made such a loving, good wife, she was a natural and quite an intellectual even though she did not have a higher education. He loved her so much that all he could do is think about her.

∼

Anne was so attractive, diligent, and sweet spirited. Harvey Ross said that you never saw her sitting idly as she was always busy. She seemed to sew for everyone in her family. One of Abraham's attractions for Ann was that she was interested in a good education.

∼

Lincoln's law partner, Herndon said he believed Abraham did love Ann Rutledge that much and he thought that Lincoln's soul was so wrapped up in that girl and Ann was his first love, and what appeared to most as the holiest thing in his life, and we know that kind of love cannot die.

∼

It would be a year after Rutledge died that Lincoln tried to carry on a courtship with Mary Owens.

∼

Some historians try to say that the only true love of Lincoln's life was Mary Todd Lincoln. This author can no way profess to be a historian or an expert on all things Lincoln but the true interests in the lives of the Lincolns have pushed curiosity to read everything available that can be found on the family and their extended families from reliable sources. It can be said in every book, and all the research conducted about Lincoln and his lady friends, it is the opinion that Lincoln's one true love was Ann Rutledge when he was sixteen and that possibly his true sexuality did not bloom until later in his life. It seems strange that the depression that remained with him for the rest of his life started after Ann's death.

∼

His reason for dating Mary Owens was to see if he could get over Ann Rutledge possibly.

∼

At a cotillion, Abraham Lincoln, 30, tried again as he came up and said to,

> *"Miss Mary Todd, I want to dance with you in the worst way."*

The very next evening, Abraham called on her at the Edwards' home. Besides, he needed a wife if he were to enter politics.

∼

The reason for dating Mary Todd had to be because her personality at the time was the opposite of his and seemed to lighten his mood. At the time of their breakup, she was probably in a dark mood, and he couldn't take it anymore.

∼

Some of her family frowned about her marrying Lincoln, and there were times Lincoln got cold feet and felt sure he would never be able to make her happy. They were engaged in 1841 and Lincoln called it the *"**fatal first of January**,"* when they broke the engagement with what seemed was started by the request of Lincoln.

∼

In all honesty, it had never been a genuine engagement as we call it today. It was a long period of dating and Lincoln had been gone several months on business, and when he came home, he knew he had to clear things up with Mary and let her know that he was not interested in marriage. The break-up was not pretty.

∼

The '*engagement*' lasted for eighteen months, and after the beginning and for a time after, Abraham seemed overwhelmed with depression and became despondent.

∾

It was quite a shock when Abraham and Mary Lincoln married suddenly on November 4th, 1842. Odd they were engaged to marry one day and the next day they were married. It seemed that Lincoln had gotten himself caught in an 'entanglement' of sorts with Mary that he could not get out of. The only solution that seemed available was that he had to marry her. Mary had seduced Lincoln on purpose so she could trap him into marrying her.

∾

When they married, Mary was 23 and Abraham was 33 years old. They were going to be married in the Edwards home and not a church, and the ceremony was given by Episcopal minister Charles Dresser.

∾

Abraham and Mary were complete opposites. Where Mary was a social butterfly, talkative and loved to be bathed in attention; Abraham was moody, got around slowly, and enjoyed being in a quiet room all by himself.

∾

Mary had always been a pampered young woman until she was married. Mary and Abraham after the wedding rented a room to live in above the Globe Tavern there on Adams Street and paid $4 a week to live there.

～

Mary had been used to luxury and spaciousness in her accommodations but oddly enough never complained about the discomfort she had to live in compared to the way she was able to live before they married.

～

It did not take long before the Lincolns found out they were to be parents. Their first child was born August 1, 1843, and they gave him the name of Robert Todd Lincoln, naming him after Mary's Dad.

～

When Robert was born, they certainly needed more space, and they moved to South Street where they rented until they could afford to buy a home with the help of Mary's father. The salary Abraham was making as a lawyer was not enough to purchase a house.

～

It was in 1844 when Mary's father bought them their first home on the corner of Eighth and Jackson Street. The house had once belonged to Minister Charles Dresser, the very minister who had performed Mary and Abraham's wedding.

～

If you add the months up, you will see that Mary must have been pregnant when she and Abraham were married or that Robert was conceived about two weeks early. He was born at 38 weeks it looks like when you calculate on the calendar of 1842-1843. When you know the background of Abrahams "*supposed sexual escapades*" and Mary's "*reportedly*" sexual encounters then it should not be surprising.

~

Two years later, in 1846, Edward, their second child was born. The money they had to live on was not that much so they could not have a maid. It made it necessary for Mary Todd Lincoln to do the cleaning and cooking for the house, and care for their two children as well as sew her and the clothing of the children.

~

On the other hand, Lincoln had his suits designed and made by a local tailor, one Benjamin R. Biddle. Some say that Mary, who had at one time had a pleasant disposition, developed a bad temper because she was so exhausted due to her change of lifestyle. Besides that, Abraham was so involved in his job when he was not out of town on the circuit.

~

It is said that Lincoln had the words inscribed on the inside of their wedding bands "*Mary & Abe - Love is Eternal*," and to those in the outside world, their marriage seemed to most that it was based on love. He stated that Mary was as pretty as when she had been a girl, and he was nothing but a poor nobody, but she still fell in love with him, and he had never fallen out of love with her.

∼

Everyone knows the Lincoln marriage was by no means perfect, and Mary and Abraham both had their faults. Mary seemed intelligent, vivacious, cultured, witty, and creative but at the same time, she was also selfish, excitable, nervous, irritable and sometimes it seemed downright mean.

∼

The Lincoln's had a neighbor in Springfield by the name of James Gourley that said the Lincolns had their ups and downs just like all families. But, always, Lincoln gave into Mary. Most men may have told their wives to quit the whining or told them to shut up. Sometimes Abe just ignored Mary's hysterics and then sometimes he would laugh at her. If Mary would continue her rant and not calm down, Lincoln would pick up the kids and leave the house.

∼

Mary's dual personality can be traced back to her childhood. Mary's cousin said that Mary had always been high strung and would be laughing like crazy one minute and then crying the next.

∼

During the White House years, staff noted it was difficult to be around her because you would never know what mood she would be in when you came to work each day. One day she would be so kind, generous, considerate, hopeful, and thoughtful and then the next day would be so unreasonable, depressed, irritable, prone to look at the dark side and see the worst in everyone.

~

Mary had such a bad temper that it made many enemies for her. When she would get offended or even angered in any way, her sweet ideas would disappear, and that stinging horrible sarcastic or satirical voice would come out in terrible bitterness.

~

Two White House secretaries, John Nicolay, and John Hay had given Mary the nickname of *"**Hellcat**," "**she-wolf**," "**female wildcat**."* They both said that her terrible nature had caused Lincoln nothing but a lifetime of unhappiness and trouble. Some try to give her the excuse that she suffered from migraine headaches during her adult life and that caused her bad mood. Research seems to tell that she had ALWAYS acted like a spoiled brat and became worse as she aged.

~

Elizabeth Keckly, Mary's seamstress, had written in 1868 that Mr. Lincoln was nothing but an indulgent and kind husband and when he noticed any faults in Mary he would excuse it like he would overlook the impulsive acts of a little child.

∼

Then again, Lincoln himself was not the perfect husband. It seemed he was always gone from home on the eighth circuit for six-eight months each year and this left Mary alone with the kids at home. It scared Mary to death because she was a nervous wreck worrying about burglars and house fires. Either Mary or Abraham would make arrangements for some neighbor boy to stay and sleep in the Lincoln home while he was away for her protection.

∼

As Lincoln's career in politics started to take off, he was away from home even more while he was giving speeches and attending campaign rallies. Mary wasn't lonely, but besides her other fears, she was terrified of thunder and lightning.

∼

Mary made no secret that she resented the fact that Lincoln was away on the circuit so much and it seemed he was the only lawyer on the circuit that was gone this much. Mary went as far as to say that if Abraham Lincoln would stay home as he should, she could love him better.

∼

It didn't seem to matter because even when he was home, Mary still complained. Lincoln stayed busy with work and politics; he avoided the social graces like wearing the right attire whether it was in or outside of the house, and he might say inappropriate things when he was out in public. It seemed like he had no filter.

∼

It seemed Lincoln did not respect Mary as the homemaker she was in their home. He often got home late for dinner or maybe not at all. He would drag in friends for dinner and not even let Mary know beforehand. He never complimented her on the food she cooked. It seemed Lincoln's marriage had loads of problems that were made worse by her horrible anger and Lincoln's withdrawal.

∼

The psychological influence Abraham Lincoln had on his wife is something that cannot be ignored. It seemed that his patience and love were the perfect hypnotics for Mary's horrible temper and erratic behavior.

∼

Someone teased Lincoln one time about Mary's tantrums, and he replied to them that it did no harm to him and it does her a lot of good, and this should hold you in never having to wonder why I am so meek. Lincoln was not submissive, but he was probably too indulgent, parental, and way too patient. Mary loved it when Lincoln called her his "*child-wife*."

PART IV

THE LINCOLN BOYS

«You cannot escape the responsibility of tomorrow by evading it today.»

Abraham Lincoln

∼

Abraham and Mary Lincoln were blessed with four boys.

∼

Edward Baker Lincoln was almost four years old, about one month before he was to turn four. The census records for that time list "***chronic consumption***" but as we know it today "***tuberculosis***" as the reason for death. Many in their family state the features were compatible with a form of hereditary cancer called multiple endocrine neoplasia or medullary thyroid cancer. It was also called "***consumption***" that was a term applied to any wasting disease. Eddie had a thick but lop-sided lower lip that was also a sign of the disease. People who inherit the MEN2B gene will 100% of the time will develop medullary cancer of the thyroid, and sometimes it will present itself as soon as the neonatal period of life.

~

Inside one of the White House guest rooms, lay 11-year-old William Wallace Lincoln (Willie) in what is now called the Lincoln Bed that is a large carved bed of rosewood. He had died at 5:00 p.m. February 20th, 1862. It seems he had died from typhoid fever that he had more than likely caught from drinking contaminated water that was supplied to the White House.

~

Elizabeth Keckly, Mary Todd Lincoln's seamstress, was the one who cleaned and dressed him for the funeral. When Abraham Lincoln looked at Willie, he would mourn about his poor boy who was too good for this earth. He felt that God had called him home. Lincoln felt that Willie was much better in heaven, but they loved him so much. It was so hard to have him die and leave.

~

Keckly watched Lincoln bury his head down in his hands and his lean, tall frame convulsed with sobs. Keckly stood down at the foot of the bed as she watched this rugged man be so moved. She said she would never forget those intense moments when the greatness and genius of the United

States President broke down and wept over his child. Lincoln walked down the hallway toward where John Nicolay was working in the White House and told him that his boy was gone, really gone! Then, Nicolay remembered seeing Lincoln bursting into tears before going ahead and entering his office.

～

Mary Todd Lincoln was in such shape that she could not be consoled after losing Willie. To make matters worse, Tad was laying in another room in the White House seriously ill. Willie had been the third boy born to the Lincoln family on December 21st, 1850; the same year that Eddie had died.

～

One of the Government official's wives words said that the White House was sad because it seemed the light and joy was gone with Willie. He was such a bright child, precocious at his age, and everyone who knew him loved him. Mary said that Willie was the "***idolized child of their household.***"

～

They allowed Willie's body to be moved downstairs to the White House Green Room where it stayed until time for burial. Doctors Brown and Alexander took care of the embalming, the same procedure that would be performed in three more years for another death that was to come.

～

Willie was laid out in a flower-covered coffin made of metal designed so it would resemble rosewood, that had his date of birth, name, and date of death inscribed on a silver plate. Friends came for paying their respects February 24th, the morning the funeral was to be held.

∼

Before the service began, the Lincolns gathered around Willie's coffin to bid their final private farewells. It was Benjamin French that supervised all the arrangements and said one of the most torrential rains and wind storms came through the city for years and it felt like the storm outside was howling with the grief like Mrs. Lincoln. She was wrapped up in her grief and not consolable. Mary Todd Lincoln stayed in her bedroom grieving during the entire funeral and the burial.

∼

The funeral started at 2:00 p.m. at the White House in the East Room, where the gilt mirrors had been covered in mourning with black fabric covering the frames and the use of white fabric covering the glass portion. Dr. Gurley of the New York Avenue Presbyterian Church officiated at Willie's service. The Lincoln's as a family attended this church, and this is where Willie had lately told his Sunday School teacher he wanted to be a preacher or teacher of the gospel.

∼

At the close of service, most of those in attendance followed the body to Georgetown to the Oak Hill Cemetery out in

Georgetown which made a long procession. Two white horses pulled the hearse, and two black horses pulled the President's carriage down the unpaved streets and then up the hill toward the cemetery.

∼

On arrival at the cemetery, they placed Willie's body in the small chapel on the grounds for a short service with Scripture and prayer. Willie would later be transferred into the Carroll Family's vault out in the cemetery's northwest section.

∼

In April 1865 Willie's coffin was again moved and placed on a funeral train and permanently placed in the Oak Ridge Cemetery in Springfield, Illinois.

∼

The death of Willie left terribly, deep scars on the entire Lincoln family. Miss Keckly said that Mary Todd Lincoln was never the same and she never went into the Guest Room where Willie died again nor did she ever enter the Green Room where they embalmed her child.

∼

It happened that on the day that Lincoln was to be assassinated that he had commented to Mary that they needed to be more cheerful because with the war and losing Willie they had been nothing but miserable.

~

Tad who was twelve when his dad died was the only child living with Mary and the only one she could force herself on for comfort at the time. Mary noted in one of her letters in November 1865 that if she could press him any closer in her heart to keep Abraham Lincoln any closer to her heart, she would because she loved the child so dearly.

~

Willie had never been given education by a tutor and Tad had never been given any early education whatsoever either, so both boys were pretty uneducated at this point. Tad had been left to enjoy and play at will as he wanted. It makes one wonder with such an educated dad as to why the boys did not start receiving a good education at an earlier age.

~

When the fall of 1865 rolled around, Mary did finally enroll Tad to a school in Racine, Wisconsin. In November Mary wrote Frances Carpenter, one of the painters who had worked and lived in the White House while painting the picture of Lincoln when he shared the Emancipation Proclamation with his White House cabinet. She also divulged that Tad was learning and loved his new studies almost as much as he loved when he had free reign around the White House playing all the time.

~

After Racine, Tad was placed in public school. Even though

he was a 13-year-old boy at that time, he still could not read, and he was large for his age probably causing him a lot of teasing in school.

~

You must remember he also had a speech impediment on top of everything else and the kids at school would call him "***Stuttering Tad.***" He had been born with a lisp and a cleft palate and his mother, Mary Todd was not consistent or either hot or cold when it came to her mothering techniques and being lenient or strict on how she treated him. It had to have been a very confusing time for Tad.

~

Robert Lincoln, in 1868 was 25 years old had taken it upon himself at the time to consult specialists regarding Tad's speech issues and there was some improvement that seems to have been made.

~

During the summer of 1868, Mary decided she should move Tad and herself to Europe where she felt Tad would get an education for less money.

~

At the time, the government was not taking care of the President's widows as our current government takes care of First Families now. Mary Todd Lincoln went to Congress and pleaded with them to start giving ex-presidents and their widows.

∼

From the research, you would have to honestly call it Mary having a temper tantrum with all the men in Congress. But, it must have worked as Congress did debate and started giving her and all President's widows to follow financial support. They were probably not very happy to find out that she was taking Tad to Europe for some education. But, it did not matter to Mary, she and Tad set sail for Germany anyway.

∼

Tad probably had no clue as to what had hit him when he started the accelerated school in Germany. Mary thought that Tad was getting so much better at his studies, but by October of that year, it was necessary for them to make a move to England because Tad needed a tutor seven hours each day.

∼

Mary got very ill in the first part of 1871, and even Tad was starting to show symptoms of coming down with something, so they went back to Chicago. Mary did get better, but Tad just kept getting worse and July 15th, 1871 Tad died, he was only 18-years-old.

∼

The newspaper "*The Chicago Tribune*" placed a notice about Tad's death the day after he died. It stated he had died at the Clifton House, where he had been ill since coming back from Europe. They claimed his reason for dying was chest dropsy. The Tribune went on to say that his first symptoms started while he was overseas, but when he arrived back to the states his condition got worse; then it got better, and then he got up during the night and had few clothes on and passed out. He went into a relapse and went into a steady downhill decline.

∼

It isn't difficult to imagine that after Eddy dying at four years old, then Willie dying, and her husband – President Lincoln, and then Tad that Mary Todd Lincoln started her mental and emotional but steady decline.

∼

Robert Todd Lincoln, the eldest son, was also known as "*Prince of Rails*" and sometimes he was called "*Bob*" but "*Robert*" detested his nicknames and had been named after Mary's father. He had been cross-eyed when a child, but as a teenager, he was reserved as well as determined.

∼

When he was sixteen, he left home and started to attend school at Phillips Exeter and then on to Harvard University. Robert did not like the public life but then again sometimes he liked the attention he would get being in the public's eye. There were times he was vain and self-centered; it made him emotionally distant from his family and mostly his father, who he spent even less time with as a child than any of his brothers.

∼

Robert was kind, reserved, and shy, but he felt like he labored in his father's shadow all the time. Robert seemed to be liked by everyone because he was sincere and generally had good sense causing him to win a degree of respect and goodwill that followed him into his personal life.

∼

Even during the time of 1861 to 1865 while Robert was a student, he became a public figure too. It seemed he could not get away from the attention of the press.

∼

It put Robert in an awkward position, especially since he was starting to hate publicity more and more. Even at this time, there was a notion going for the presidential son starting to form. If he could hold himself apart from the prying gaze of the public eye, he was snobbish or arrogant, but if he gave the appearance of trying to capitalize on the position as being the son of a President, he would be damned for that too.

∼

When Robert was a child and into his early youth, he said his dad was gone all the time. Abe Lincoln would be out attending circuit courts or giving political speeches. When Robert turned sixteen, Abraham Lincoln, Robert went away to New Hampshire and then on to Harvard Law School and then by that time Abraham Lincoln was president. Robert said that when his dad was president, he never had more than ten minutes of quiet talk with his Dad.

∽

Robert interrupted his Harvard Law School education to briefly serve in Grant's army as he was criticized because he was not serving in the Army. Robert wanted to enter the army even earlier than he did, but Mary Lincoln could not stand the idea of him joining since he was the only child she had left.

∽

Abraham Lincoln told Mary Todd Lincoln that many mothers had given up every one of their sons and here is our son not more dear than the sons of other mothers.

∽

Abraham Lincoln went on to say to Mary that the services of all men who loved their country should be required to serve in this war. Mothers and Fathers should be liberal and not selfish in their views to let their sons serve.

∽

On the morning that President Lincoln would be assassinated, Robert Todd Lincoln ate breakfast with the family.

Robert and the President were looking at a picture and in the newspaper of General Robert E. Lee. Lincoln told Robert Todd Lincoln that he was glad the war was finally over and that Robert was finally safely back home. He went on to tell Robert it was time to trade in his uniform and go back to college and finish his three years he had left and by the end of that time, he should know if he would be a good lawyer or not.

∼

Lincoln seemed happier than he had in a very long time. Robert, being Lincoln's eldest child, lived to be quite old and died at the age of 82 in the year of 1926.

∼

One thing can be said for sure; Abe and Mary Lincoln had that mutual affection and interest in everything their boys were involved in and more importantly, the welfare of their boys.

∼

The Lincolns did have their quarrels, and sometimes they got pretty hectic and they, of course, became exaggerated by the wagging tongues.

∼

Mary had fits of temper, recurring headaches, and a terrible sense of loneliness and insecurity.

PART V

THE MADNESS OF MARY LINCOLN

«Whatever you are, be a good one.»

Abraham Lincoln

∼

Mary Lincoln's problems did by no means start after she married Abraham Lincoln. Oh no, they started when she was a pampered child and would not get her way. She would throw her fits of temper tantrums (or so it seemed at the time) until someone would give in and let her have her way.

∼

There is not enough room in many books to discuss the madness of Mary Lincoln and all her peculiar ways. Mary was in the spotlight, and lots of tongues liked to wag.

~

It seemed that both Mary and Abraham suffered from psychological wounds that would cripple them emotionally and might have contributed to all the difficulties they would be put through later as husband and wife.

~

Mary's family, the Edwards, were an influential family living in Springfield down the street from Mary and Abe Lincoln. Mary had always been considered popular with the young men while there in Springfield and had been courted by several aspiring politicians and lawyers. Mary was educated, witty, smart, graceful and great with her conversation and entertaining ways.

~

Mary could be described as the weight of about 130 pounds, and average height. She seemed to be built compactly, had a round face, dark-brown hair, and blue-gray eyes. She acted proudly, appeared vivacious, somewhat pretty and could also speak French.

~

Mary had a quick wit and seemed to make a quick judgment of all men and what their intentions might be. Most of the time it seemed she could be charming with her manners, but if you ever offended her, she could eat your liver out by being sarcastic and bitter. With her height, temperament, background, and education – in every part of her being she was the exact opposite of Lincoln.

∽

In Springfield, there was a teenage Matilda Edwards that Abraham Lincoln chased while in his early thirties. Matilda caught the attention of all the men in town in 1841.

∽

It is said that Matilda Edwards broke more male hearts than any other girl who had ever lived in Springfield. Matilda always said that if the men liked her, it would not be any fault of hers.

∽

The story is that Todd had lots of suitors, but not apparent that she chased anybody else besides Lincoln. Another attorney, Orville Browning, felt that Mary Todd did all the chasing of Lincoln. It seems that in all the conversations it had come out that Lincoln had confessed to Mary Todd that he was really in love with Matilda Edwards.

∽

Mary Todd seemed to be anxious to marry Lincoln. Lincoln appeared to be a man who felt that '***marital bliss***' was only an oxymoron.

∽

It was in 1864 when Lincoln gave pardon to a soldier who was going to desert to return home so he could marry his sweetheart. As Lincoln signed all the appropriate documents, he told the intercessor there on behalf of the soldier that he was not punishing the young man because probably in less than twelve months he will wish Lincoln himself had not given him the pardon. There is lots of evidence that makes you think that Lincoln hated his marriage as much as he felt the soldier would hate his eventually.

∽

There were always visitors at the White House, but there was one very notorious visitor from New York that no reputable woman should ever be seen with because of his reputation. He had traveled in Europe, and no one knew where he got his money to do so. He paid lots of attention to Mr. and Mrs. Lincoln but more so to Mary Todd Lincoln.

∽

He was at the White House so much that it was being noticed by all the President's friends. When there was a reception held by Mary Lincoln he was the first one to show up. At any informal dinner, he would show up. Everyone else would be gone, and he would still be there. The White House servants saw him in and out all the time.

∽

There were those that heard Wycliffe complimenting Mary Todd Lincoln on the way she looked and on her dress in such a way that she would blush and tell most men to be gone from her. Instead, she was accepting of Wikoff for her guide in social etiquette, personal requirements, welcoming company for visitors in her salon, on drives, and other domestic arrangements.

∼

There was more than one time he was seen riding in the President's coach with ladies along Pennsylvania Avenue. He never tried to hide his presence. It did not look appropriate or complimentary for the President's family. Some papers were making it look scandalous.

∼

There was contempt for Wikoff, and it was widespread. While lounging one late September in President's Park, others were enjoying Marine Band Music and if you looked up at the grand portico of the White House, there stood Mary Todd Lincoln and no one else by her side but Wikoff.

∼

Mary Todd Lincoln was found to be very vain and wore her dresses more revealing at the top to show her breasts and have a longer train than any fashion demanded. She was prideful about her bust and neck, and it bothered the President how she wanted to show off her body in her beautiful clothes consistently.

∼

One historian by the name of Edwin Emery noted that there

were parts of Abraham Lincoln's first speech he was going to give to the regular session for Congress in December of 1861 that suddenly appeared in the Herald newspaper the same morning Lincoln was going to give his talk.

∼

John Hickman, the Chair of the House Judiciary Committee turned it into an investigation of where the leak began. It was easily traced to who else but Wikoff and the sordid mess was hushed before the facts were made public.

∼

Many felt that Wikoff obtained the speech from Mary Todd Lincoln. Wikoff was arrested, and attorney Sickles put a deal together to get the White House Gardner by the name of John Watt to admit to memorizing the messaging when he saw it in the President's Home office.

∼

In the end, it was found there was a group in New York that wanted Lincoln out of office, so they hired a man who was penniless to use as their tool for their needs. One couple furnished him with the instructions and the money he needed to carry out his terrible deeds. He was sent to infiltrate the White House, flatter the ladies and find out everything. Wikoff would send quick bulletins regularly to his bosses in New York letting them know how he was proceeding in the dirty work.

∼

Robert Lincoln was always pushed into the background but was the son that wound up fixing everything for the family. Robert tried to say it started July 2nd, 1863 from a carriage accident, and while riding toward Washington coming from the Soldier's Home, the carriage's driver's seat came detached, and it threw the driver out on the ground.

∼

The horses got frightened and started running frantically along Rock Creek Road, and Mary leaped from the carriage to save herself.

∼

Report of the accident stated that Mary was battered, stunned, and bruised, but she had no broken bones, and the injuries did not appear to be dangerous. She had a wound at the back of her head that had been caused by a sharp stone. President Lincoln sent a telegraph to Robert who was studying at Cambridge and told him not to worry and that his mom was only mildly hurt by her fall.

∼

There were emotional effects that went along with the physical injuries. Mary's nurse felt the accident had been an assassination attempt toward the President because the driver's seat had been sabotaged. It made Mary's fears for her husband's life even worse.

∼

The President gave little time to Mary because he was so busy managing the war. Robert sure did not see his mom and decided to ignore his dad's telegrams. Both of the neglects probably made Mary feel more disconnected from her family as now she only had Tad to give her the undivided attention.

∽

Mary went to her bed; President Lincoln again hired Rebecca Pomroy, the one nurse who had come to care for Mary after Willie and Tad's death. Mary's benign wound became infected. It took three weeks before Mary finally got out of bed.

∽

Mary had always suffered from bad migraines for all of her entire adult life. After the accident, it seemed like the headaches were becoming more frequent.

∽

Robert Lincoln later shared with his aunt that it seemed his mom had never completely recovered after her head injury. It appeared that he felt it had an impact on her mental health.

∽

It seemed that for Mary and her intense grief with Willie's death, it seemed to couple with all the effects of her head injury, didn't cause her to go crazy but it brought her closer to the edge. Emily Helm, who was Mary's half-sister, happened to notice in 1863 that Mary seemed to be excitable, nervous, and in constant fear that more bad things were going to happen in her life.

∼

Emily had also written in her diary that told of a night when Mary had come to her bedroom while smiling with her eyes brimming with tears and said to her that Willie had visited her during the night. He has been coming to see me every night, and he stands down at the foot of my bed. He doesn't always come alone as Eddie sometimes is with him. She told Emily that seeing him gave her great comfort.

∼

You cannot know for sure, but it could have been Mary's first actual psychotic symptoms. In Mary's later years she would only sleep on one side of the bed so Lincoln could sleep on the other side.

∼

In 1880, even though she had Robert entirely from her life, she went ahead and put in the newspaper that Robert was going to be President. It gave her a slight reprieve of losing her son and losing her position in society.

∼

It seemed that from 1863 until Lincoln died that Abraham and Mary drifted apart. She stayed away from him because she was afraid he might bring up subjects like her extravagant spending and all her debts. He never wanted to confide in her because he didn't trust her judgment, mental health and who she might tell. He never wanted to share any sensitive info with Mary. There was little left for them to have to talk about.

∽

Lincoln had a friend, Orville H. Browning that said he remembered Mr. Lincoln told him on multiple occasions that he worried all the time about what Mary might do to bring him some disgrace. He had to continually be on the watch for Mary being jealous of how his wife might misinterpret his talking with other women.

∽

It seemed that during their later married years together, Mary had probably tested and strengthened all of the President's innate qualities of patience and tolerance.

∽

It was in 1875 that she was officially given the diagnosis of insane. Mary had always been extremely emotional, and when Willie died, it damaged her. Mary locked herself in her room for weeks, which caused Robert Lincoln to ask Mary Todd's older sister, Elizabeth to come and stay with Mary at the White House.

∽

Mary was not able to look at anything associated with Willie. Aunt Elizabeth left after two months, and then President Lincoln hired a nurse. Mary got rid of all of Willie's cloth, possessions and never let any of Willie nor Tad's friends, (mostly Holly and Bud Taft), to come to the White House.

∾

After Abraham Lincoln's death, all Mary wore was what they called "***widow's weeds***," but before that time the had accrued a massive wardrobe of expensive gowns that she would certainly never wear again. To raise money, she decided that she would sell some of her elegant dresses.

∾

It all happened before the Smithsonian Institute started the First Ladies Collection. Mary Todd Lincoln went to New York while using an assumed name and she took her dressmaker Elizabeth Keckley with her. They went to resale shops and thrift stores trying to find buyers. Nobody wanted to pay the money she wanted for the dresses.

∾

Mary Todd Lincoln got entangled with a pair of dishonest salespeople that sold her a bad bill of goods. They had guessed who Mary was, and convinced her that it would be best to sell the dresses at auction. Mary grabbed the bait.

∾

It got more complicated, and Mary Lincoln went back to Chicago and left Lizzie Keckley to manage the sales. The auctioneers made it all worse by talking Mary Lincoln into giving what they called '***personal letters***' they could show to any potential buyer. It was more or less glittery blackmail.

∼

The auction of Mary's dresses became a massive scandal and was all over the newspapers and so humiliating. The event became a total failure, and even worse Mary had to put out more than $800 to get her dresses back.

∼

Mary Lincoln had a predisposition for psychiatric illness along with a life of emotional and mental trauma that led her to be committed to the insane asylum. There was one psychiatrist that diagnosed Mary suffered from a bipolar disorder.

∼

There were so many factors in Mary's life that could have contributed to all of her strange habits and her declining health mentally. Whatever happened, if only Mary Todd Lincoln had just encouraged the President to stay at home April 1865 that evening, Mary's life and of course those of many others could have turned out a lot differently. Sad but true that Mary was holding Lincoln's hand when he was shot. I cannot be sure about anyone else, but for this author, that alone would be enough to make anyone crazy.

∽

Abraham Lincoln understood Mary's mental problems and what he had to do to keep her stable. It seemed like he knew just what to do and how to talk her down every time.

∽

After Lincoln's death, Mary became Robert's responsibility. There is much documentation as to why and how he dealt with Mary and the reason he had Mary committed, how he responded to when she tried to commit suicide, and even how Mary had plotted to murder Robert. Robert was not a bad son. He also agreed to have her released from the Psych Hospital eight months before she was set to be set loose.

∽

While living in Chicago, the Hotel would call Robert and ask him to please come and get his mother as she was running around naked again in the Hotel lobby.

∽

Mary had such horrible spending habits even when the country had no money. Mary would get the White House bookkeepers to juggle the books for her and lie to Lincoln about how much she was spending.

∽

There is another explanation, one that her doctors wanted to hide for as long as possible, and that was that Mary and the President both had syphilis, and possibly Mary's delusions were a result from her nerve cells degeneration that was carrying information to her brain. It was all caused by syphilis. Mary had displayed all the primary symptoms of syphilis: dementia, weight loss, knife-like back pain, impaired coordination, and eventually blindness leading to death.

∼

The syphilis story came from Lincoln's law partner in Springfield, a William Herndon, who in some of his private notes in 1891 stated that in 1835-36 Lincoln had gone to Beardstown and while there become involved in a passionate moment caught the disease from a girl.

∼

After Mary Lincoln had died of what they were sure was a stroke on July 16th, 1882 there was an autopsy that also revealed she had a brain tumor. No one had any idea or what type of tumor it was or how long it had been growing there. It could have been an explanation for her eccentricities or mood swings.

∼

As Mary aged, she became nearly blind and had lost a lot of weight. She had diabetes, and it could have been a cause as well. We will not know for sure whether the blindness was from diabetes, cataracts, syphilis, the brain tumor or any other causes.

PART VI

QUESTIONABLE RUMORS ABOUT LINCOLN

«You can fool all the people some of the time, and some of the people all the time, but you cannot fool all the people all the time.»

Abraham Lincoln

∽

Everyone had heard the rumors that when a young man in Springfield, Illinois, Lincoln shared a bed for four years with Joshua Speed. Speed was possibly the closest friend Lincoln had ever had.

∽

It seemed like the longtime affair he had with Joshua Speed was visible when you read their letters after Speed moved to Kentucky to get married, and Lincoln was getting nervous about marrying Mary Todd in Springfield. Each was terrified about their wedding night.

∼

If you desire to know more dirt about Lincoln and Speed after they wed, you will not find it in this book. When Lincoln was age 28, he had been admitted to the lawyer's bar; Lincoln moved from New Salem to Springfield that seemed like a sprawling metropolis with its '*1500*' people. When Lincoln got there in the spring of 1837, he immediately went to the General Store, and to his disappointment found out that just sleeping on a mattress with a pillow and some linens would cost him $17. That was all he could afford at the time, and it would require him sleeping with another man. Joshua Speed who he had never met before.

∼

It seemed that the people in Springfield, Illinois did not like talking about Lincoln. They had no intention for telling good things about Lincoln but if cornered in private would sure tell you what his weak areas were. They would be glad to tell you all his weak points and the damaging facts they saw every day and knew about. In secret, the people of Springfield seemed to hate him.

∼

There was a fellow lawyer by the name of Henry Whitney who felt that Lincoln seemed to be courting him all the time. He went on to say that Lincoln told him that to have sexual contact was the same as a *'harp of one thousand strings.'*

~

If this is all Lincoln said it could be taken in many ways. He may have meant this as talking about a woman. This statement could have been misconstrued unless we are not given the full magnitude of the entire conversation.

~

It is also noted that Henry Whitney was known for *'stretching'* the truth and making his stories more interesting. So, no matter where this tidbit comes from, even a reliable source and directly from Henry himself does not mean it is the truth.

~

Most want to know how the contacts took place. There was a hint given by one Billy Greene that was sharing a bed and was a grammar teacher and living with Lincoln around 1831 in New Salem.

~

Greene himself described Lincoln as having an influential figure as being attractive to him, and he commented on Lincoln's powerful thighs. What was called *'femoral intercourse'* was considered to be a useful substitute and orgasm whether mutual or else, was between the other's firm thighs?

~

There is much evidence that there was an 'affair' that began on September 8th, 1862, when the President would go to the Soldier's Home (always when Mrs. Lincoln would go to New York to do some serious shopping).

~

Lincoln would send for Captain David Derickson so he could get to know him. Derickson had deep-set eyes, five foot nine, had a prominent nose and thick black hair. He was 44 years old, so that made him nine years Lincoln's junior. When the affair started he had nine children by two different wives; a grown son that served with Company K. Others were too quick to note that when the two shared a bed, Derickson always wore one of Lincoln's nightshirts.

~

We must remember that Lincoln also did visit the whore in Springfield at the boardinghouse that wanted three dollars. Lincoln did not have that much and asked for credit, but the girl finally gave it to him for free.

~

One must wonder how many times syphilis was spread. Lincoln thought he had been treated, but at that time there was no real treatment for syphilis. They had no idea of how it could travel and settle in the brain.

~

So, if Lincoln were rising in the political world in Illinois, it would be necessary for him to take a wife and get busy with a family. But then, he broke off that engagement. After the breakup, he took to his bed. He wrote a poem that he titled "*Suicide*," that was published in the local newspaper in Springfield, and then was secretly cut from the file copy.

∼

So, the truth about whether Lincoln was a heterosexual, homosexual, or bisexual remains to be validated entirely. It will be left for each person who reads this book to decide.

∼

Let me add as a last note to this chapter: There is nothing new under the sun. In other words, no matter what the century lived, there is nothing that has not happened before.

∼

No matter what color someone's front door is painted or how beautiful their house may be, no one can ever know what is going on behind that door.

PART VII

RACING TOWARDS POLITICS

«Nearly all men can stand adversity, but if you want to test a man's character, give him power.»

Abraham Lincoln

~

It was early in Lincoln's life when he was a freethinker and a skeptic. Lincoln felt that his reputation had been tainted because he had complained one time of the '*church influence*' and they used it when he jumped into the political race.

~

In 1846 when Lincoln was running for Congress he had some handbills printed denying that he had never in his career spoke intentionally with disrespect about religion. He did not stop there, however, as he went on to say that he did believe in a doctrine of necessity –

> *'the human mind is always impelled to act, or held to rest by some other power over something that the mind has no control.'*

All through Lincoln's life, he believed in enigmatic signs, dreams, and omens. When he grew older, and even more after he became president and came face to face with all the responsibilities brought on by the Civil War, he seemed to develop what appeared to be a profound sense of religion, and he personified his belief of the necessity of God.

~

He started to look at himself humbly as an 'instrument of Providence' and to look at all of the ancient times as the enterprise of God.

~

It was in 1862 when Lincoln wrote that during this present Civil War it is possible that God has a purpose that is something entirely different from what either side is fighting for, but yet the individual objectives that work as they do are one of the best ways to effect God's purpose.

~

It is said that Lincoln was fond of the Bible and he knew it thoroughly and then you will find other researchers that will say when it came to the Bible, he was not much of a believer.

∼

Lincoln was also a fan of Shakespeare. When in private conversations he would use lots of Shakespearean references and discuss the problems of their dramatic interpretation with substantial insight and would recite some long passages from his memory with some rare feelings and understanding.

∼

Andrew Jackson was the U.S. President when Lincoln first entered the race of politics. Lincoln agreed with Jackson's ideas for the common man, but he did not agree with how they felt the government should divorce itself from the economic enterprise.

∼

Whenever it came to the legitimacy of the government, Lincoln later said he was to do for the community of people what they needed to be done but are not capable of doing it for themselves in individual and separate capacities.

∼

Daniel Webster and Henry Clay were two of the prominent politicians of that time that Lincoln admired the most. Both politicians advocated by using the federal government's powers so they could encourage business and be able to develop the United States resources by using a protective tariff, a program for internal improvements for external transportation improvements, and use the national bank. Lincoln felt that the West and Illinois desperately needed the aid for development economically, so from the beginning he started associating with the Whigs, the party of Webster and Clay.

∼

Being a member of the Illinois Legislature for which he had been elected four times beginning with 1834 and ending in 1840, it was Lincoln that started devoting his time to big projects to construct with the use of state funds for highways, canals, and an entire network of railroads and other infrastructure for the country.

∼

The Democrats and the Whigs passed an omnibus bill for all of these developments but when the panic of 1837 and all the depression of businesses brought down the crash of almost all of them. While he was in the legislature, he started letting it be known that he opposed slavery, that he was no longer an abolitionist.

∼

It was in 1837 when there was a mob murder of one Elijah Lovejoy, who was against slavery and a reporter for a newspaper of Alton, the Illinois legislature presented resolutions that condemned the abolitionist societies and defended the position of slavery in all of the southern states by the

Federal Constitution. Lincoln would not vote for the recommendations.

∾

Lincoln and another congressional member wrote a protest that stated, on the one hand, and slavery had been founded on lousy policy and injustice and also on the endorsement of the abolition doctrines that tends to increase instead of decreasing the evils.

∾

During his one term in Congress (1847-49), Lincoln was the only Whig from Illinois, and he was giving little attention to any of the legislative issues at hand. He did propose one bill for gradual and reimbursed freeing of the slaves in the District of Columbia. Since it was to only take effect with the approval of '*free white citizens*' living in the district, it made the abolitionists mad, and slaveholders were never given serious consideration.

∾

During this time Lincoln devoted a lot of his time to getting elected as president. He had found one issue and one candidate during the Mexican War. With what he called his '*spot resolutions*,' Lincoln argued with the statement of President Polk that Mexico were the ones that started the entire war by spreading American blood all over American soil. With other members of the Whig party, Lincoln was able to condemn Polk and the whole war effort and vote for supplies to carry on with it. All this time, he was laboring for nomination and getting elected war hero Zachary Taylor.

~

When Taylor had success at election polls, Lincoln was sure he would be named the commissioner to the general land office in the form of a reward for services during his campaign, so he was disappointed, to say the least when he did not get the job he had bet on.

~

He criticized the war and was not popular with the voters in his district. At age 40, he was frustrated with all politics, and it looked like he was at the end of his career in politics.

PART VIII

ON THE ROAD TO THE PRESIDENCY

«Give me six hours to chop down a tree and I will spend the first four sharpening the axe.»

Abraham Lincoln

∼

It would be about five years before Lincoln would take any part in politics again, and then it was when a new crisis caused him to reemerge and rise to statesmanship.

∼

Stephen Douglas, one of Lincoln's rivals, in 1854 took through Congress a bill that would reopen the entire area of the Louisiana Purchase for slavery, and it would allow people to settle Nebraska and Kansas to make their decision by themselves as to whether to enable slaveholding in the territories.

~

The Nebraska-Kansas Act then provoked the violent opposition in the state of Illinois and other countries located in the old Northwest. It developed the Republican Party while it was speeding along with the Whig Party toward its way to being disintegration.

~

Lincoln was soon to be a Republican as did many other homeless Whigs. It did not take long before some of the prominent Republicans out in the East wanted to attract Douglas into the Republican camp, and along with him tried to pull his Democratic group to the West. Lincoln said he would have no part of it. It was Lincoln that was so determined that it would be him and not Douglas who should be the Republican to lead his state.

~

It was Lincoln who challenged incumbent Stephen Douglas for the current open Senate seat when 1858 rolled around, and then the debates started, and they continued throughout Illinois that made history that shall never be forgotten.

~

Both of the men were excellent debaters and great stump

speakers, but entirely different in the way they looked and how they dressed. There was the plump but short Douglas who spoke with a loud voice and used graceful gestures that easily swayed his audiences.

∼

Then you had the homely, tall, anorexic looking Lincoln that moved around awkwardly and his voice was shrill and piercing. Lincoln's speeches and prose he used were concise, eloquent, free of wordiness, and compelling as he spoke.

∼

One thing when you backed off and viewed the situation, Douglas and Lincoln were not that much different when it came to the heat of arguing over politics.

∼

They shared the same views on proslavery and abolition. But then there was Lincoln, not Douglas, that insisted Congress should exclude slavery in the territories.

∼

Lincoln did not agree with Douglas that believed the territories were unsuited for the slave economy and there was no legislation in Congress needed for preventing slavery from spreading.

∼

In one of Lincoln's more famous speeches, he announced that

> "A house that was divided against itself will not stand."

Lincoln felt that there was no way the government could stand permanently in half free and a half-slave state. At that time he predicted that the country would eventually be either all slavery or all non-slave.

∿

Lincoln said, again and again, he would insist that every U.S. citizen should insist on their civil liberties whether they were black or white because they were all at stake.

∿

Depending on his audience at that time, he would reassure his viewers that he would in no way allow citizenship for the black population or even believe in giving equality of all races.

∿

At one crowd in Charleston, Illinois he told them he had never been in favor of making the jurors or voters of the blacks, nor letting them hold any office, or allow them to marry whites. Lincoln went on to say that there were physical differences in the two races which he felt would bid forever the two tracks that lived together when it came to terms of political and social equality.

In the end, it was Lincoln that lost to Douglas in the election. The outcome didn't surprise Lincoln, but it caused him to go into a deep depression. One thing for sure was it had brought Lincoln into the national spotlight, and they were soon talking about him being a presidential candidate for the 1860 elections.

It has always been thought Lincoln wore a stovepipe hat because it was his favorite hat style. But it was more than a hat to him. For Lincoln, it was his portable filing cabinet where he kept his notes, his letters, and his money.

May 18th, 1860 Lincoln was nominated at the Republican Convention in Chicago. He gave up his law practice, quit making his stump speeches and gave in full time to his presidential campaign.

Lincoln was working with a united Republican party while the Democrats were divided with a total of four candidates total and Lincoln won the election November 6th. Lincoln got NO votes in the Deep South and over the country no more than 40 out of 100 in the entire region. The popular votes were distributed as such that he was able to win a decisive and clear majority with the electoral college.

~

When Lincoln was president, Mary thought she was a hotshot and had genuinely arrived at her rightful destiny.

~

After Lincoln was elected and before he was inaugurated, South Carolina withdrew from the Union. To keep other Southern states from making the same mistake; there were different compromises developed in Congress, and the most important one was the Crittenden Compromise.

~

Before Mary Todd and Abraham Lincoln had even moved into their new home at the White House, they were facing a crisis as six other states besides South Carolina had pulled away from the Union and shaped the Confederate States of America. Things were already about as bad as they could get.

~

The North and the South started focusing on Fort Sumter located in Charleston Harbor, South Carolina. The fort, while still being built, was filled with U.S. troops under the supervision of Major Robert Anderson. The Confederacy automatically claimed it as their own. Lincoln saw trouble immediately from Springfield; he requested that Winfield Scott, general in chief for the U.S. Army and told them to get prepared to retake or hold the forts as the case might require before or after the inauguration.

~

Lincoln had barely got in office when he received word that at Fort Sumter that unless it were withdrawn or supplied they would be starved out completely. Generally, Scott and others were trying to urge Lincoln to abandon Fort Sumter.

~

While on the other hand, there were many Republicans who felt if they showed any sign of weakness, it could bring total disaster to the Republican Party and the entire Union.

~

Lincoln then ordered two expeditions, one for Fort Pickens and the other for Fort Sumter. Before the Sumter expedition, Lincoln sent someone as a messenger so he could tell the governor of South Carolina that if they did not wait for Lincoln's expedition arrival, the authorities from the Confederates would present to Major Anderson and demand for Fort Sumter's evacuation immediately, and the governor refused. Then on April 12th, 1861 during the early morning dawn hours, the Confederates out in the harbor started firing. The Civil War had begun.

~

When Congress and Lincoln met July 4th, he told them those who were assailing the government had begun their conflict toward them. Then the Confederates accused Lincoln of being the aggressor. The Confederates told the story that Lincoln had been intelligent about the way he had maneuvered them to fire the first shot so they would be the ones who started the war. Some historians feel these facts are distorted. Lincoln wanted to preserve the Union, but so that he could do that he had to keep the Union and take his stand against the South. Lincoln decided he might as well take his biggest stand there in Fort Sumter.

∼

When the war began, Lincoln thought it would be a short one. Once the firing at Fort Sumter began, Lincoln asked the state governors to send troops. Virginia along with three states of the upper South did respond by becoming part of the Confederacy.

∼

He then blockaded the Southern ports. All the above decisions were some of the first decisions that Lincoln made as to the country's commander in chief for the U.S. Navy and Army. Lincoln still desired a plan with a command system to carry all of this out.

∼

General Scott told Lincoln to avoid battle with the Confederate troops in Virginia so he could get control over the Mississippi River and tighten the blockade for holding the South with a massive crush.

∼

Lincoln seemed to have little confidence in the plan Scott

wanted to use that was so Anaconda like. He felt the war had to be aggressive if they were going to win it well.

∼

Lincoln's two closest assistants would tell you that the White House at that time sitting on the Potomac was not the right place to be located as the stench coming from the Potomac wafting in from death was nauseating, and the odor lived with you night and day. You could never get away from it. The summer heat made it worse, and the windows of the White House had to be left open because of the heat.

∼

Lincoln felt he had the world on his shoulders. Lincoln realized so many people hated him, and he had lost two of his children at this point, and he had already lost the love of his life? Death surrounded him every day as he looked out across the front yard of the white house. Who would not feel depressed?

∼

Lincoln overruled Scott by ordering a full-on advance at the Virginia front that resulted in the defeat and to rout out the federal forces there at Bull Run on July 21st, 1861.

∼

After many days of sleepless nights, Lincoln sent out memos of their military policy. His thought was the armies needed to move forward in a concurrent pattern on several fronts and needed to move so to hold on and use the support of the Unionists in Kentucky, eastern Tennessee, western Virginia, and Missouri.

∼

Along with the naval blockade, it made up the essence of Lincoln's strategy. Being a war leader, Lincoln used the same style he had used as a politician and describing himself in a way that he was never ashamed to accept.

∼

Lincoln had rather react to the problems that other people created rather than make new policies and try to lay out the long-range plans. In total honesty, Lincoln would write that he never claimed to have control over any event, but he did confess that events that had happened did control him.

∼

Lincoln was nothing but a practical man, he was flexible and agile mentally, and if even one decision or action were unsatisfactory in practice, he would be willing to work with another.

∼

While Lincoln would hesitate on imposing any of his ideas on any of his generals, he would also experiment with his command troops and the entire organization. Lincoln accepted Scott's resignation in November 1861, when he decided to put George McClellan in charge of all the armies.

∼

A few months had passed when Lincoln got disgusted with the slowness of McClellan, and he chose to demote McClellan to only commanding the Army of the Potomac alone. He then started having questions about other plans that McClellan had developed for the Peninsular Campaign.

∼

After the Seven Days' Battles, so they could capture Richmond, Virginia on June 25th thru July 1st, 1862, it failed, and Lincoln ordered him to give them up. Lincoln tried another succession of commanders who came to serve on the army from Virginia – John Pope, Ambrose Burnside, George Meade, and Joseph Hooker and even McClellan again. But, as time went by Lincoln became disappointed with each of them.

∼

For a while, Lincoln put Henry Halleck, as a general in chief who would give the advice and serve as the go-between with the field officers but at the same time did not like making important decisions.

∼

For almost two years the Federal armies did not have the unity of command. General Halleck, President Lincoln, the War Secretary Edwin Stanton were acting like an informal council of war.

Lincoln, would transmit his official orders thru Halleck, communicate directly with his generals, send personal ideas out in his name. For the generals that might be opposing Robert E. Lee, Lincoln would suggest the object would be to obliterate Lee's army, and drive the invader off from Northern soil and not to capture Richmond.

∽

Lincoln finally decided to start looking out West for a leading General. He had admired the leadership skills of Ulysses Grant in the state of Mississippi. It was nine days after Vicksburg had surrendered on July 4th, 1863 when Lincoln sent a '***Thank You***' note for his invaluable service for our country.

∽

In the note, Lincoln sent Grant an admission of an error he had made. He told Grant he had thought Grant would bypass Vicksburg and then head on down to Mississippi instead of crossing over the river and then turning back to move on toward Vicksburg so they could approach Vicksburg from behind.

∽

March of 1864 found Lincoln promoting Grant on to lieutenant general and allowing him to have commands for all the federal armies. Lincoln had finally found someone who had subordinates like Philip Sheridan, George H. Thomas, and William T. Sherman that could make things happen per Lincoln's concept on a large-scale and coordinate the offensive that still had to be followed through.

∼

During 1855 while Lincoln was writing to Joshua Speed, his old friend, he remembered a steamboat ride they had both been riding on the Ohio River together about 14 years prior. He asked Joshua Speed if he remembered that while riding from Louisville, Kentucky down to the opening of the Ohio River there were ten or even a dozen slaves, on board all shackled together with irons. Lincoln said when he saw the sight, it was a torment to him.

∼

Lincoln was reluctant at first for adopting a policy for abolition. He had several reasons to be hesitant. When he was elected, it was on a platform that pledged there would be no interference with the slavery in the states.

∼

At the same time, Lincoln worried about the potential difficulties for incorporating almost what would be four million blacks, if and when they would be freed, into the U.S. political and social life.

∼

When Generals David Hunter and John C. Fremont, inside their military departments sent out the proclamation that there would be freedom for all those slaves who worked for disloyal masters, Lincoln decided to revoke the declaration.

∼

Congress passed the confiscation acts of 1861 and 1862, and Lincoln kept from fully enforcing the provisions that authorized him to start seizing slave property.

∼

Due to the response toward the antislavery sentiment, Lincoln decided to come forward with his plan about emancipation. He proposed that the slaves would be freed by the action of the state, then the slaveholders would be reimbursed, and then the federal government would help in sharing the financial burden. The process of emancipation would be gradual; the men to be freed would be colonized abroad.

∼

Congress agreed it was willing to vote that it would give the funds necessary toward the Lincoln plan, but there were none of the neighboring slave states that wanted to participate, and in any case, there were few African Americans who were in a leadership position that wanted to see their people sent abroad.

∼

Lincoln wanted his original plan to be a success, but he issued a final Emancipation Proclamation on January 1, 1863.

It decreed that only those sections of the country that were under Confederate control, and not to the slave states that were remaining loyal or to the occupied areas of the Confederacy.

∼

Whether indirectly or directly this proclamation did bring freedom while the war was going on to less than 200,000 slaves. It was a substantial significant symbol. It also showed that Lincoln's government added freedom to the reunion as far as a war aim, and this attracted the liberal opinion in Europe and England for increased support in the Union cause.

∼

Lincoln himself was not sure if the step he had decided to use was constitutional, except for use as a temporary measure during the war. Once the war was over, the slaves were all given their freedom by this proclamation but would have run the risk of being re-enslaved and had nothing else that was done in confirming their liberty.

∼

So, there was something else done by way of the Thirteenth Amendment that was added to the Constitution, but Lincoln played his part in bringing to the country his change with the fundamental law.

∼

By the chair of the Republican National Committee Lincoln urged the Republicans to start including a plank for amendments with its platform of 1864.

∼

The plank as adopted, said that slavery had been the reason for the rebellion and that the President's Proclamation aimed a "***blow of death toward the large evil***," and a constitutional amendment to be able to "***terminate and prohibit forever.***"

∼

At the time Lincoln was re-elected, the Republican majority held in Congress increased, Lincoln felt justified, and he had a mandate coming from the people for the Thirteenth Amendment.

∼

For the new Congress that was chosen, it was mostly a Republican majority, would not meet until the lame duck session of the past Congress during winter 1864-65. Lincoln would not wait.

∼

With Lincoln's resources for persuasion and patronage with certain Democrats, he got the necessary two-thirds vote before the session would end. He celebrated as the amendment was sent out to all the states for possible ratification, and he celebrated once more when Illinois first led and others states joined one by one to act favorably with it. Lincoln never lived to rejoice in its adoption.

∼

People felt that Lincoln deserved his reputation he had earned as the Great Emancipator. Lincoln strengthened with the practical demonstrations where he gave respect for the dignity and human worth no matter the color of skin.

∼

For Lincoln's last two years of living, he more than welcomed the African Americans as his friends and visitors in such a way as no president had ever done before. If there was a reception in the White House, African Americans were just as welcome to come through as whites and allowed to shake Lincoln's hands. To this Mary, Lincoln was having fits as they were messing up her carpets. Lincoln did not care. The carpets belonged to the people.

PART IX

WARTIME POLITICS

«I am not bound to win, but I am bound to be true. I am not bound to succeed, but I am bound to live by the light that I have. I must stand with anybody that stands right, and stand with him while he is right, and part with him when he goes wrong.»

Abraham Lincoln

If Lincoln were to win the war, he needed popular support. It seemed for the Union that Lincoln was the President that possessed that rare political skill of appealing to other fellow politicians. He had a way about him that would smooth over their differences and still hold on to the loyalty of the men who were antagonistic with one another.

However, the opposing party was alive, well, and secure. It consisted of a membership that held the '*War Democrats*' and the '*Peace Democrats*' who were sometimes called the '*Copperheads*,' and there were even some of them who would collaborate with the enemy.

∼

After the war, Lincoln had to make a lot of hard decisions, and he justified his actions for the reasoning that one had to allow some sacrifices and parts of the country's Constitution.

∼

Lincoln had a friend by the name of Orville H. Browning that felt the arrests that had been ordered by Lincoln were '*arbitrary and illegal*,' but were probably doing more harm than they were doing any good, causing more weakness instead of strengthening the U.S. Government. Still, Lincoln stood firm and defended his actions. He argued that the Constitution gave the reasoning for suspending the liberties '*in instances of an Invasion or a Rebellion, when the people's safety may be at risk.*'

∼

Lincoln had inside his very own party, those who were confronting some of the factional divisions and their conflicts that were causing him nothing but trouble just like the Democrats. It was true that when it came to the economic plans that Lincoln and most of his Republican party agreed.

With Lincoln approving, the Republicans put into place a law that the essentials were things he had promoted from earlier in his political career like a national banking system, construction of a railroad to reach the Pacific Coast, a protective tariff, and use of federal aid for improvements internally for the United States.

∼

Within the Republican Party, there were still two factions: The '*Conservatives*' and the '*Radicals*.' Lincoln leaned toward the Conservatives, but some of his friends were hanging out in the Radical section. It made it hard for Lincoln, but he had to work hard to maintain control and leadership over both sides.

∼

When Lincoln appointed his cabinet, he chose those who believed as he did and those who were direct rivals for his 1860 nomination. He felt that it would give fair representation for each critical party.

∼

It sounds like an uphill battle when you realize he included Seward who was an outstanding Conservative, and Salmon Chase was a die-hard Radical. Lincoln was quick like a fox and was able to quickly pull his cabinet through crises and managed to keep the opposites held together until Chase finally resigned in 1864.

∼

Everyday Lincoln was dealing with more big issues such as factional uprisings breaking out in Congress. It seemed the most substantial issues were when it came to 'reconstructing' the South. The states of Arkansas, Tennessee, and Louisiana had pretty much already been recovered by the government's armies. It was late in 1863 when Lincoln decided to introduce his 10% plan. It would acknowledge that when a new state government would form that 10% of the voters who qualified had taken their oath for future loyalty toward the United States.

∼

Of course, the Radical section rejected Lincoln's proposal were way too lenient, so they passed it through Congress by attaching it to the Wade-Davis Bill. That way they could have let the readmission and remaking of each state after there had been a majority had taken their loyalty oath. Lincoln then pocket-vetoed the bill; all its authors later published a 'manifesto' so they could denounce him.

∼

Since Lincoln was already considered the candidate for the Republican party to be re-elected for President, with the Wade-Davis Manifesto, it signaled to the movement inside the party to get rid of Lincoln as the Republican's nominee. Lincoln was waiting patiently, not saying anything and hoping the action that was planned would collapse; but then when it happened, the party was more divided than ever.

~

There was a rival Republican candidate by the name of John C. Fremont, who was nominated a lot earlier by some splinter group out in the field. There were the leading Radicals that promised to get their hands on Fremont to withdraw if Lincoln would get the conservative postmaster general, Montgomery Blair to resign.

~

So, eventually, Fremont left and then Blair resigned. The party finally reunited in time for the 1864 election. It stayed the same in 1864 as it was in 1860, as Lincoln was his strategist for the campaign. He even had a hand in managing the Republican Speakers' Bureau, then advised the state committees on what their campaign tactics should be, fired and hired government employees so he could gain the support of the party, then he did whatever he could to empower all the sailors and soldiers that could to vote. He found that a majority of citizens who wore red uniforms voted Republican. Lincoln won that election by a vast, accessible majority (55%) over Democrat General George McClellan.

~

The Democrats used for their platform in 1864 a peace conference and an armistice, so, therefore, the prominent Democrats or Republicans demanded Lincoln should heed the Confederate offers of peace, no matter how irregular they appeared.

The Conservatives started protesting to him about the implication that the war should go to free all slaves. In his usual inaugural address, Lincoln promised he would be liberal with the pardons if only the South would stop the war, but he kept insisting on a reunion for a condition if there was any peace arrangement. In his Second Inaugural Address, he expressed the embodiment of his policies by his famous words *"**with malice toward none; and charity for all.**"*

~

Lincoln's terms did not satisfy the Radical Republicans or the Confederate leaders, so it boiled down to the one fact that there was no peace possible until the Confederacy defeat was final.

~

As with all things government, either now or then, when the Civil War did end, Lincoln and his policy for the South's defeat was nowhere evident in the details. Lincoln did continue to feel and believe that their primary objective and priority needed to be in restoring the '*seceded states*,' back to their original place in the Union as quickly as possible.

~

Lincoln had no real fix or uniform program for that region as a whole. States like Tennessee and Louisiana, Lincoln could continue in urging the acceptance of any new governments to set up under the 10% plan he had designed during the Civil War.

~

For states like North Carolina and Virginia, Lincoln was willing to fall back on the older rebel governments for a temporary means so they could transition from a war setting to a situation of peace. Lincoln was noted as in opposition against 'no strangers' could govern the South.

~

Lincoln felt that education should be offered to blacks and whites and allowed to go to the same schools. He also thought that the blacks that were extremely intelligent and those who fought in the war should be able to vote.

~

When it came to reconstruction, Lincoln and those who fell out as extremists in his Republican sector stuck out like a sore thumb in the early part of 1865, worse than they did one year before.

~

Some Radicals started demanding there should be a time of military supervision over the South, the transferring of political power from the plantation owners to their prior slaves, confiscating the estates and dividing them between the free men.

∽

April 1865 found Lincoln starting to change some of his ideas in regards to some respects, and this helped in narrowing the gap between him and the Radicals. Lincoln went ahead with his permission for assembling the rebel legislature in Virginia; Lincoln approved the principle of Stanton's ideas for the military occupation of the Southern States.

∽

When the Cabinet met April 14th, Attorney General James Speed said that Lincoln seemed to be leaning toward the radical position.

∽

It did not matter because Lincoln kept his eye on what his goal had been all along and that was to restore the United States to a single nation all under the original Constitution. Ending slavery was to be secondary to the first goal. The 13th Amendment that banned slavery through all of the United States passed after Lincoln had pulled enough political strings and granted all the favors needed to get the required "*Aye*" votes — already failing one time in the House, before all of Lincoln's backroom meddling and negotiations. Thaddeus Stevens had to say that the biggest measure of the 19th century would be that this Amendment had been passed by the use of corruption, abetted, and aided by the man considered to be the purest in America.

PART X

STILL MAD ENOUGH TO MURDER

«No man has a good enough memory to be a successful liar.»

Abraham Lincoln

∼

April 14th, 1865, John Wilkes Booth was 26 years old and an advocate for slavery with his ties to the South and the flashy son of the most prominent theatrical families during the 19th century decided he would murder Lincoln.

∼

The assassin that killed Lincoln died April 26th, 1865 was killed near Port Royal, Virginia.

∼

Booth had been number nine out of ten kids born to actor Junius Booth. It was felt he had great potential for the theatre at an early age but was also beginning to show an emotional instability. On top of it all, he was having an issue that made it hard for him in accepting his brother Edwin's claim to fame as a rising actor of that day.

After John had found no success in Baltimore Theaters during 1856, he played some of the minor roles he found in Philadelphia until the year 1859, and he then joined a The Shakespearean stock company there in Richmond, Virginia. John became widely known while on tour in the Deep South during 1860 and the demand remained all through the Civil War. He even had a turn as the lead in "William Shakespeare's *Richard III*" while in New York City during 1862.

Booth being a strong supporter of the Southern cause hated Lincoln. He wanted slavery. By the fall of 1864, Booth started plotting an abduction of none other but Lincoln himself. Booth recruited several men to work with him, and during the winter they worked out several different scenarios. Several attempts they tried, failed, so Booth decided to destroy Lincoln no matter what it would cost.

Booth heard about Lincoln going to the theatre on April 14th, 1865 to see the play '*Our American Cousin*' at Ford's Theatre there in the capital. Booth gathered his band of bad boys and gave everyone their assignments, and they had even planned on murdering the Secretary of State, William Seward. Booth wanted to kill Lincoln himself.

∼

At 6:00 P.M. John Wilkes Booth went into the empty theatre and tampered with the outside door to the presidential box so he could jam it shut once he got inside. Booth came back during the third act to locate Lincoln and those with him and found them without any guards.

∼

When Booth got inside the theatre box, he pulled out his .44 caliber pistol and shot Lincoln behind his left ear. He fought shortly with Major Henry Rathbone and then jumped over the railing while shouting. He landed/fell hard on the stage which broke a bone in his left leg. There seems to be some argument that some feel the injury did not happen until later.

∼

Booth made his escape through the alleyway with his horse. Trying to kill Seward was a failure, but Lincoln died the next morning.

∼

Booth met up with one of the other in his gang, a David Herold. Booth went on to flee through the state of Maryland. He only stopped to have his leg fixed by a Samuel Mudd, who was supposedly a doctor in Maryland who later would be convicted of conspiracy.

∼

There was a massive manhunt that followed, and a $100,000 reward fueled it. Herold and Booth hid out for days near the Zekiah Swamp in a thicket of trees still in Maryland state.

∼

April 26th the Federal Troops were on the scene at a farm there in Virginia, south of Rappahannock River. Booth was supposed to be hiding out in the tobacco barn there. Herold gave up before they set the barn on fire. Booth still refused to surrender.

∼

Booth was shot, not for sure if, by himself or a soldier, he was carried to the farmhouse porch, where he died. A doctor who had operated on Booth in the past year, ID'd his body, and then it was secretly buried. Four years later they had it reinterred. As always there was no evidence to support that it was John Wilkes Booth that had been killed.

PART XI

ROBERT & HIS DEALINGS WITH MARY TODD

«A man watches his pear tree day after day, impatient for the ripening of the fruit. Let him attempt to force the process, and he may spoil both fruit and tree. But let him patiently wait, and the ripe pear at length falls into his lap.»

Abraham Lincoln

∾

After Lincoln died, Robert resigned from service, and he and his mother, Mary Todd Lincoln moved to Chicago, Illinois where he settled in to practice law.

∾

Robert married a Mary Harlan in 1868, and they had three

kids, but their one and only son died when he was a teenager.

~

His mom's wild spending led him eventually to him having her placed in an insane asylum during 1875. When Robert's aunt, Mary's sister, found out where she was at, she went to the insane asylum and had her released to her care.

~

Robert was more public-spirited, and he served under President Chester Arthur as the Secretary of War in 1881-85, President James Garfield, and later on, he served as the Minister to Great Britain in 1889-92.

~

Robert's presence while working during the assassinations of both President William McKinley and Garfield seemed to make him self-conscious about fatalities when attending presidential functions.

~

For a while, Robert served as the president of the Pullman Company. While there he led a quiet life before dying in 1926, always trying to protect and preserve his father's memory.

~

Robert was known as a hard-working man, disciplined, confident, strong, self-aware, generous, proper, a real gentleman, kind, witty, and very intelligent. At the same time he could be impatient with others and despised laziness and ignorance, did not like deception and lies when it came to selfish and dishonorable people, and if you ever offended him, he was good at holding a grudge just like his mom's family.

Mary's Charlatans

∼

It seemed Mary Todd started making trouble for President Lincoln as quickly as they moved to Washington. She had, you might say, strong opinions of other people. If she were not able to change Lincoln's mind herself, she would try different routes to get her way.

∼

She was always meddling about how to distribute some of the minor offices and tried to interfere with the assignment of Cabinet members. The people who were around her knew how to flatter her to gain control and influence her.

∼

After Willie Lincoln had died, her situation got even worse in the spring of 1862. Elizabeth Keckley, her seamstress, felt to help Mrs. Lincoln feel better would be for her to see a medium or a spiritualist. These people sure did not improve Mrs. Lincoln's mental stability.

∽

Mary and Abraham Lincoln were communicating with those who had passed on seemed natural to them. President Lincoln even once asked one of the Union officers if he had ever caught himself talking to the dead? He confessed to this young officer that he had found himself involuntarily talking to Willie as if he were next to him ever since Willie had died.

∽

The period President Lincoln was laying in a state before they took him by train to Springfield, Illinois, Mary Lincoln was so frantic in her suffering they had to leave her in her bed.

∽

Mary was obsessed with loving and especially more so with worrying about her children and husband. As it turned out, she had a good reason for the worry. She lost three of four sons, and then her husband being killed. Maybe it was more premonition that caused her fear.

∽

Mary's letters always told about the gossip going on in Washington and Springfield, Ill detailing the news about her children, some of the political activities taking place, and her expressions of pure longing for companionship and intimacy.

~

There were Nicolay and Hay who had never gotten along with Mary Lincoln. They worked and even slept in the White House, but never ate their meals in the White House.

~

Because Hay and Nicolay were such close friends to Lincoln, they sometimes would go to the theater if Mary was away from Washington. Hay and Nicolay had been friends forever; before Hay had gone away to Brown University. They both had literary goals, and both admired the President.

~

Both men were always ready for late night talks to discuss public policy or some political jokes with the President. May 14th, 1864 in Hay's diary he had recorded that the President had come in last evening and told them about his retirement of the enemy at Spottsylvania and the Unions pursuit.

~

Hay had complimented him on the underpinning he had left, and Lincoln made the comment that he weighed 180 pounds. The stating of that fact is essential due to the situation of his health revealed later in this book.

～

President Lincoln became extremely depressed over all the death of all the young men who had given their lives for this cause. Lincoln would sit by a window at one end of the White House for hours and hours at a time trying to figure out how to hang himself from the oak tree outside without anyone noticing until it was too late. (Of course, no one at this point knew that Lincoln had had syphilis for quite several years now and one of its symptoms could be depression.) There were some nights that his two closest friends and advisors would take turns sitting with him so he could not harm himself.

～

Both secretaries got along well with Robert Todd Lincoln when he came home from Harvard on vacation. Mary alienated Nicolay and Hay quickly, and they called her the 'hellcat' for all her demands. When William Stoddard, the presidential aide prepared to be leaving the White House to go to Arkansas in the fall of 1864, it was John Hay that told Nicolay that he had no idea what they would do after Stoddard was gone. He said that the two of them by themselves could not manage Mary Lincoln. Stoddard was the only one who could ever handle her.

PART XII

LINCOLN'S FINAL HOURS

«When I do good I feel good, when I do bad I feel bad, and that's my religion.»

Abraham Lincoln

∾

The assassination is probably one of the saddest events known to American History.

∾

We find that the morning of April 14th, 1865 was good Friday, and Lincoln got up in a good mood. It had been on Sunday, April 9th that Robert E. Lee had surrendered to Ulysses S. Grant. The famous truce was signed at Appomattox, Virginia at the Court House and signaled an end to the United States most terrible Civil War.

~

The Lincolns decided to celebrate the end of the war they would go to Ford's Theatre and see *"Our American Cousin."* Lincoln had asked that General Grant and his wife go with them that evening. Grant told him they could not as they were on their way to see their kids in New Jersey.

~

What appears to make it more ominous is that Secretary of War at the time, Edwin Stanton, begged Lincoln not to go to the theatre as he had a bad feeling of a possible assassination. Mary Todd Lincoln did not want to go either, and she was having another one of her bad headaches. Even Mr. Lincoln fussed about being so tired and exhausted. But, he said, an evening out for comedy would probably help them feel better.

~

Lincoln had such confidence in his bodyguards and the fact that they would keep him protected that he shrugged off everyone's warnings and even invited Major Henry Rathbone and his fiancée, Miss Clara Harris.

~

Lincoln's primary bodyguard, Ward Lamon did not go to the play, and John Parker was sent instead. John Parker, a police guard, was known by everyone for his like of whiskey, and he was supposed to be protecting the President? Where was

Parker when the President was murdered? He had left his post outside the President's box at the time of intermission to go to the Star Saloon to help with his craving for alcohol.

∼

During the 3rd act, Mary and Abraham were laughing and holding hands when a man ran into the box that was now unguarded. The intruder as you know was the actor, John Wilkes Booth, a Confederate sympathizer. Booth used a Derringer pistol to shoot into the backside of the President's head. Rathbone immediately tried to take down Booth, but Booth was able to overpower him by making a slash to Rathbone's arm with a dagger.

∼

Many have different versions of what he said after Booth shot the President. Some are:

> *"The South is Avenged?", "I have done it!",*
> *"Revenge for the South!"*

One thing known for sure is that Booth jumped from the President's theatre box onto the stage and as he jumped caught his boot spur on the curtain and caused him to break his left shin. (As you know from above there is some argument to if he broke his left shin at this point or later.) Somehow Booth limped away and made his exit out the stage door, initiating the largest manhunt in American history.

∼

When you think about it, even being in a coma, the real story is the sadness of the hours of pure agony the President had to endure before he expired that early morning April 15th.

∼

Through scientific evidence produced in a prominent medical school in New York today, we find even after being pronounced dead the soul stays in the body for quite some time. Until Lincoln was dead, his soul was still there and could hear all that was being said around him. He had to know he was dying that his vision/dream he had told someone about had indeed come true. While trying to do his very best as the President of the United States, there was still someone who hated him so very much they were willing to take any risk to kill him.

∼

When the audience started crying out that the President had been shot and to catch the murderer, the first doctor to get to the President was Charles A. Leale a 23-year-old Army Captain, he had only graduated with his medical degree six weeks prior.

∼

Dr. Leale was immediately able to assess that the bullet entered the skull behind the left ear and tore into the left side of the brain. Dr. Leale sent out for water and brandy, and by the time he got to President Lincoln, Abraham was already paralyzed, eyes closed, and in a coma. Lincoln's breathing was difficult and noisy but only intermittent. By placing a finger on Lincoln's right radial pulse, there could be no movement of the said artery.

∽

When Leale's fingers had passed over Lincoln's head during the examination, he noticed a *"**large firm clot**"* just one inch under the curved back line at the occipital bone. Dr. Leale removed the clot by wiggling his finger in the hole that the pistol ball had made and realized it had gone into the brain.

∽

Today, this maneuver seems shocking; but at that time doctors had no idea about sterile technique nor microbiology, and it was the standard method used to examine gunshot wounds. It was clear that it was a mortal wound and no going back.

∽

When Lincoln's breathing seemed to be a bit better, and the doctor could get some water and brandy down his throat two more physicians had shown up. The three doctors decided to move the President across the street to a boarding house. He was moved to the upstairs in a Union soldiers room who had stepped out for the evening.

∽

Because Lincoln was so tall, he had to be placed on the bed in a diagonal position. They removed the foot of the bed so he could lie in a more comfortable position. Windows in the room were opened up and everyone except for the doctors, Mary Todd, Robert, their son, and some of Lincoln's devoted advisors, were cleared from the small room.

∼

The doctors tried to get the lead ball out by probing around inside the wound with some surgical instruments and of course unwashed hands. Since surgery of the brain was not a specialty in Lincoln's time, the surgeon's only hope was to keep the wound open so the blood might keep flowing freely so it would not compress Lincoln's brain further and causing more injury. Their efforts, of course, did nothing and as the morning ticked by Lincoln kept declining. It is appalling at the least at what they did not know about medicine at that time. However, from what is described of the damage done inside Lincoln's brain by the bullet, even today there would doubtedly have been any '***bringing back***' with today's medicine.

∼

It was 6:40 a.m., Dr. Leale said that his pulse could not even be counted; it was so intermittent. He could only feel two or three beats that were followed by a long intermission. His breathing got even shorter, and his expirations were longer and so labored while being accompanied by the guttural sounds.

∼

Ten minutes later, Dr. Leale stated that the respirations would cease at times and everyone would look at their watches in the event it might be his last, and then the silence would be broken by an inspiration very prolonged, then followed by a loud expiration.

∽

The President was not in good health, to say the least, and who are we to say that he had that much time left in his remaining presidency. Most people have no idea that during his final living years that there was a high probability that Lincoln did have cancer of his adrenal glands. We also do not know who had the carrier gene for the thyroid cancer which their one son had died. He had syphilis that he thought he had been cured from but certainly was not. Apparently, it had reached its latent stages by the symptoms Lincoln was exhibiting.

∽

All three doctors examined him, and it was written that President Lincoln had breathed his last at 7:20 a.m. and his spirit fled to God who had given it.

∽

Secretary of War, Stanton saluted his friend and fallen President and uttered that now our President belongs to the ages. Here lies the perfect ruler of men that the world has ever seen.

∽

Three days before he died, Abraham had told his bodyguard Ward Lamon that he had dreamed a funeral had taken place at the White House in the East Room. While he was dreaming, he asked a soldier standing near his casket about who it was that was dead. The soldier informed him it was the President because he had been killed by an assassin.

∽

Mary Todd Lincoln was so beside herself she could not even attend his funeral. To her, life was over. It would be a month before Mary Lincoln could pull herself together enough to get packed and leave the White House. She was in such a state the doctors refused that she be allowed to be moved.

∽

At almost five o'clock May 22, 1865, Mary Lincoln, Tad, Robert, and Lizzie Keckley descended the public stairway and entered a horse-drawn coach.

∽

Let us remember that the real purpose of writing someone's biography is to make the person fully known to those who read all the facts of the hero or heroine that should be told. The whole of their life needs to be told, even the smallest events that include the way they felt, their thoughts, determinations, and deeds. It should be the duty of the writer to make sure everything is told, the good and bad as it makes up the character of the person and what turned them into who they were in life and how their life contributed to the world in which we live. Everyone has a purpose and leaves their imprint on others lives, sometimes, far into the future.

PART XIII

CONCLUSION

∾

If nothing else, the biography of Abraham Lincoln proves that in the United States a man can come from humble, 'very humble' beginnings and through hard work, believing in themselves and perseverance still has the chance to make a difference for themselves, others, their country, and the entire world.

∾

It takes honesty and courage to stand up against the many who may speak out against you as you try to do the right thing. You must keep placing one foot in front of the other and keep living your life honestly, and eventually, others will see that you are a man of honor and look to the future to serve those who have looked up to you.

~

Lincoln did not live in the lap of luxury even though his wife tried to do so. Lincoln did not mind living and socializing with the poor and the blacks as he came from such unfortunate beginnings and he understood their different plights.

~

Did the Civil War and all the effects afterward solve everything? Unfortunately, it seems it did not. Different races seem to be still not able to get along with each other and feel one is more superior or that one race has been through more than the other. Each race has its battle; it feels it is fighting. Sadly enough, we were all created in the same image and race, creed, nor color should not enter into any of it. The Civil War only set the slaves free, but it did not cure the problems of division, it only started them and made them worse.

~

Lincoln, despite the rumors and the ugly lies, will always be looked upon as one of the greatest presidents in the succession of all presidents of the United States. He will not be looked down nor remembered for some of his peculiarities. Today, it is the way of the world, is it not?

~

The difference now is we have telephones, Instagram, twitter, facebook, televisions, iphones, ipads and all the other types of communication devices that we know what happens around the world the minute it happens.

~

The big difference today? Today there is so much backbiting, lying, greed, dishonesty and we seem to be living in a world of entitlement that it makes some of us so very tired. In Lincoln's day, yes there was backbiting, lying, greed, deception, and killing but it was not as easy as it is today to know about everyone else business without all the modern conveniences.

~

Maybe that was the best time in history to have lived? Let us remember the real purpose of writing someone's biography. The job of the author is to help the reader know better the person we are writing about. To read all the facts that should be told and their imprint on this life. The whole of their life needs to be told, even the smallest points that include the way they felt, their thoughts, their ideas, determinations, good and bad deeds. The writer must make sure it is all told, the good, sad, and the unfortunate as it makes up the character of the person and what turned them into who they were/are in life and how those experiences caused their life to contribute to the world in which we live. Everyone has a purpose in their time on this earth, and each leaves their imprint on others' lives in some way, sometimes that imprint may not be noticed until far into the future. Remember, we have but one chance of traveling through this life to make a difference.

Strengths of Lincoln:

- Calm and enduring and seemed to keep everything held inside. Very patient with all who approached him. Thought before he would answer.
- He was a person who could talk to anyone, any age, any color and understand what they were telling him.
- He had a secure connection with the poor people because he had lived that life and Lincoln knew what it was like to be the poorest of the poor.
- He never felt or acted like he was better than anyone else.
- He built his presidential cabinet with his friends and his enemies. You can keep your enemies close so you can watch him.
- He was keen on strategies for war and for mediating between the parties in Congress to get the votes he needed.

Weaknesses of Lincoln:

- He was not strong as a father figure. He let his children and his wife Mary run over him and get their way.
- It seemed like a young man he was very good at sewing his seed or his oats with the young ladies. It also seemed it was hard for him to turn down an offer by some of the women, Mary Todd for sure requiring them to get married quickly and

have a son almost exactly eight months and two weeks to the day they married.
- For the rumors that he also liked gay men, it seemed he did not try very hard to keep this a secret. Everyone around him seemed to know about his '*trists*' while they lived in Washington and they turned their heads.
- He had syphilis which was untreatable at that time, and it made him extremely fatigued, his weight loss, and the depression he suffered.

PART XIV

FURTHER READING

More Good Reads About Lincoln

~

- Abraham Lincoln: A biography of an American President, by Anthony Moss
- Team of Rivals: The Political Genius of Abraham Lincoln, by Doris Kearns Goodwin
- A. Lincoln: A Biography, by Ronald C. White Jr.

Copyright © 2019 by Kolme Korkeudet Oy

All rights reserved.

No part of this book may be reproduced in any form or by any electronic or mechanical means, including information storage and retrieval systems, without written permission from the author, except for the use of brief quotations in a book review.

YOUR FREE EBOOK!

As a way of saying thank you for reading our book, we're offering you a free copy of the below eBook.

Happy Reading!

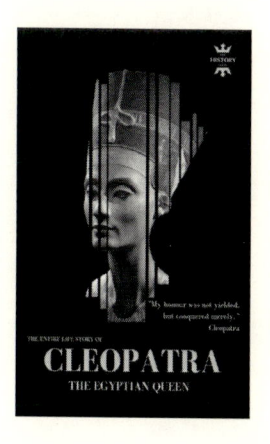

GO WWW.THEHISTORYHOUR.COM/CLEO/

Made in United States
North Haven, CT
07 November 2022